Giraffes Count

Written & illustrated by Carolyn Paradise

Goose River Press
Waldoboro, Maine

Copyright © 2019 Carolyn Paradise

All rights reserved. No part of this book may be reproduced in any form without written permission from the publisher, except by a reviewer who may quote brief passages in a review to be printed in a newspaper or magazine.

Library of Congress Card Number: 2019946961

ISBN: 978-1-59713-209-1

First Printing, 2019

Published by
Goose River Press
3400 Friendship Road
Waldoboro ME 04572
e-mail: gooseriverpress@roadrunner.com
www.gooseriverpress.com

Dedication

To my dear grandson, Benny, who inspired me with his love of giraffes and to my beloved, incredible children, Leila, Kiira, and Spencer who I've been privileged and grateful to share my life with.

A special thanks to Will and Randi for the use of their Africa pictures, as well as to my wonderful Casco Library friends.

One giraffe says hello.

Two giraffes bend their heads low.

Three giraffes stand
in clouds.

Four giraffes hide
among boughs.

Five giraffes form a herd.

Six giraffes carry tickbirds.

Seven giraffes eat green leaves.

Eight giraffes stand tall as trees.

Nine giraffes glow in sun.

Accompanying Facts

One: Giraffes are gentle, curious creatures. They enjoy interactions with people, once they are familiar with them, especially if there are treats.

Two: While giraffes can go without water for several days, relying on moisture in plants, drinking can be precarious since they have to be in an awkward position. Usually giraffes will take turns standing guard while others drink.

Three: Ancient people thought giraffes with their long necks had their heads above the clouds and were therefore closer to the spirit world.

Four: The blotches or spots on a giraffe's body help them blend into the landscape.

Five: Giraffes are usually in groups though they may separate in search of food. Their senses are so keen that they are aware of their companions as much as a mile away.

Six: Tickbirds, or oxpeckers, help giraffes by eating ticks and other parasites that prey on them. The birds also clean wounds on the giraffes, preventing infection.

Seven: Giraffes eat leaves, especially acacia, which are too high for other animals. Their tongues are able to delicately pull leaves and avoid thorns. Some farmers appreciate the giraffes' ability to keep invasive species in check.

Eight: Giraffes are the tallest animals on earth standing up to 15 feet tall. Even a newborn giraffe is almost 6 feet tall.

Nine: Every giraffe has its own distinct pattern of blotches. Among the nine species of giraffes the shapes and size of blotches vary.

Ten: Giraffes sleep very little. They usually doze for just a few minutes at a time while standing up.

About the Author

Carolyn Paradise has always loved nature, books, and art. She has incorporated her passion for these in her many years of working with children as a librarian, teacher, coach, and therapist. The plight of animals all over the world has concerned her greatly and when she learned how endangered giraffes were and what beautiful creatures they are, she wanted to honor them and draw attention to these mystical, magical beings.

She invites parents and children everywhere to learn about the work being done to save giraffes and how we can all help.